CONTENTS
MARMOTTAN – CLAUDE MONET MUSEUM

Cover:
Claude Monet,
Water Lilies, Evening
Effects, 1897-1898,
oil on canvas, (detail).
73 x 100 cm.

Pages 2-3 and 75:
Claude Monet with
the duc de Trévise,
in is second studio
at Giverny, 1920.
© Roger-Viollet.

Above:
Claude Monet,
Waterloo Bridge,
c. 1900, pastel,
30 x 47 cm.

PREFACE

by Arnaud d'Hauterives, Perpetual Secretary of the Académie
des Beaux-Arts, Director of the Marmottan-Claude Monet Museum.

**The Marmottan Museum, situated between the Ranelagh gardens
and the Bois de Boulogne, is a former hunting lodge, which originally
belonged to Christophe Edmond Kellerman, the duc de Valmy.** Acquired
by Jules Marmottan in 1882, it was transformed the following year into a
private townhouse by his son Paul. An art collector and historian, Paul concentrated his research on the Consulate and Empire periods. In 1910, he enlarged
his home so that he could exhibit his collection of paintings, furniture
and bronzes from the Napoleonic era. At his death in 1932, he bequeathed his
mansion and all the works within to the Académie des Beaux-Arts, with
the aim of creating a museum. There was no reason to think that this museum
devoted to the Empire would become, over the years, one of the world's
greatest Impressionist museums.

In 1957, Madame Victorine Donop de Monchy, only daughter of Dr. Georges
de Bellio, decided to give the entire collection inherited from her father to the
Marmottan Museum. Dr. Bellio, a homeopathic doctor of Romanian origin,
treated a number of painters, including Manet, Monet, Pissarro, Sisley and
Renoir. The purchase of his first Monet in 1874 marked the beginning of a
long friendship with the master of Giverny. His collection included, among
other works, the seminal painting entitled *Impression: Sunrise*.

It may have been this first donation that inspired Michel Monet, the painter's
second son, to bequeath the property of Giverny to the Académie des Beaux-
Arts, and the works inherited from his father to the Marmottan Museum, thus
giving the museum one of the most important collections of Claude Monet
paintings in the world. Many of them were inspired from his garden at Giverny;
this works prefigured the large *Water Lilies* in the Orangerie.

The architect Jacques Carly, then curator of the museum, constructed a
basement room to exhibit the painting. In 1987, the collection formed by Henri
Duhem and his wife Mary Sergeant entered the museum, forming an admirable
complement to the two other bequests. Henri Duhem, a painter and friend of
the post-Impressionists, was a passionate art collector, like Gustave Caillebotte. He amassed an extremely representative collection that included
paintings and pastels by Boudin, Carrière, Corot, Gauguin, Guillaumin, Monet,
Renoir, Lebourg and Le Sidaner. Also in the museum is the extraordinary
series of illuminated manuscripts collected by Georges Wildenstein and given
to the museum by his son Daniel. This donation includes 228 French, Italian,
German, English and Flemish works.

Since its creation in 1934, the Marmottan Museum has continued to expand
its collection through donations and bequests, the most recent of which came
from Annie Rouart. The aim of the foundation bearing her name and that of
her husband Denis Rouart, grandson of Berthe Morisot and Henri Rouart,
is to promote the works of Berthe Morisot, Edouard Manet, Edgar Degas,
August Renoir and Henri Rouart in their collection.

Left to right:
French school,
Jean Bourdichon
(c. 1475-1521),
The Kiss of Judas,
miniature
on parchment,
20 x 13.5 cm.

Southern French
(or Catalan) school,
The Crucifixion,
c. 1215, miniature
on parchment
from a psalm book,
16.7 x 11.8 cm.

Collection of Illuminations

by Caroline Lesage

"If you would like to learn about and love art, go see the great masters as often as you possibly can. When you can finally feel them, touch them with your spirit, savor their colors again and again, then you will start to understand." This was how Georges Wildenstein (1892-1963), one of the most famous art dealers of our century, explained his passion for art. Early on, he was taken to art galleries and major European museums by his father, Nathan Wildenstein, who was also a dealer for such collectors as Gulbenkian, Rothschild and David-Weill. For his fourteenth birthday he received two illuminated pages from a fifteenth-century manuscript and four years later, in 1910, he purchased a thirteenth-century *Crucifixion* from Maggs, a large London bookstore. This was the beginning of a collection that "Monsieur Georges," as he was called at Drouot, built up for more than 50 years.

In the eighteenth century most of the miniatures, which were highly prized by collectors, were torn from psalm books, books of hours, missals, antiphonaries and so on. The Wildenstein collection, which does not include any entire works, is representative of this period when books were cut up. Examples include a complete page removed from the *Hours of Etienne Chevalier* – the Chantilly Museum has magnificent fragments of this same book – and a miniature by Jean Perréal, *Alchemy* (stolen from the Saint Geneviève Library in 1850). Following the advice of Bernard Berenson and Charles Sterling, Georges Wildenstein created an exceptional collection that includes more than 300 medieval and Renaissance illuminated pages; the French and Italian schools are particularly well represented.

In 1971 his son, Daniel Wildenstein, was elected to the Académie des Beaux-Arts. He then offered his father's collection to the Institut de France and in 1980 presided over its installation in the Marmottan Museum, which hung the works exactly as they had been displayed in his father's office on the Rue de la Boétie.

FRENCH SCHOOL

liofi cofefftone feram folema celebrem? benerates cu fuma lecti

Left to right:
Jean Fouquet
(c. 1420-77/81),
*Episode in the Life of
Vrain*, (exorcizing in
Notre-Dame de Paris),
miniature on
parchment from
the *Book of Hours of
Etienne Chevalier*,
22 x 14 cm.

French school,
1491-93, *The
Amiral de Gravile
Hunting Wild Boar*,
miniature on
parchment, page
from the *Terrier of
Marcoussis* created
for Louis Malet,
lord of Graville and
admiral of France,
37.6 x 27 cm.

Jean Perréal
(1455-1530),
Alchemy, the only
miniature
illustrating the poem
written in 1516
by Jean Perréal:
*Nature's Lament
to the Wandering
Alchemist*,
18.1 x 13.4 cm.

These three illuminations from the French school illustrated fifteenth- and sixteenth- manuscripts. Books of hours, popular in the fifteenth century among wealthy families, were collections of pious texts and prayers that were recited at canonical hours of the day. They were often elaborately decorated, like this page from the *Hours of Etienne Chevalier*, in which Jean Fouquet created a composition in perspective, the first of its kind in France. The "Terriers" on the other hand, were detailed inventories of a lord's property with a list of the taxes due by the inhabitants; these were used by the nobility. They are precious records of life in a domain, and often express the naturalistic style of the fifteenth century, as, for example, in this *Wild Boar Hunt*. Finally, *Alchemy*, a miniature by Jean Perréal, depicts the lesson given by Nature (a nude and crowned winged woman) to the alchemist, who represents the humanism of the Renaissance: the philosopher's stone must be *opus nature* and not *opus mecanice*.

ITALIAN SCHOOL

In fifteenth- and
sixteenth-century Italy, the
art of illumination
borrowed the forms and
new pictorial vocabulary
of the Renaissance.
The Mission of the Apostles
is still essentially
Byzantine and Gothic in
style; only the
playful rabbits seem to
be free from the
static composition.
In *The Baptism of
Constantin*, a page from a
collection of songs,
there is a balance in the
proportions between
the figures and the space
containing them,
while the scene offers
a perspective
toward the outside.

It is an extremely symbolic work, because the baptism of the Roman Emperor Constantin by Pope Sylvestre made Christianity the religion of the Empire. The superb ornamental capital letter, which consists of elements of classical architecture, prefigures the richly decorated margins of animals, foliated script, *putti* and architectural designs of the Italian Renaissance. The border around *The Dream of Saint Romuald* is a tentative example of this development.

Left to right:
Empire furniture:
armchairs and chairs
in front of a
flat mahogany desk
by Pierre-Antoine
Bellangé.
Photograph: G. Fessy.

Portraits of Jules
(1829-83) and
Paul Marmottan
(1856-1932).
© Bibliothèque
Marmottan.

Jules and Paul Marmottan: Collectors

The Marmottan Museum stands in the heart of the Ranelagh gardens, in a triangle of greenery in the lovely Muette neighborhood. The bright chandeliers are just visible through the high windows of the mansion, which still looks like a private residence. Indeed, the former owners are in a place of honor just inside the door: a bust of Jules Marmottan faces another one of his son Paul. Under the sculpture of the latter is an inscription in marble: "Because I was told that all of my collections deserve to be kept forever for the instruction of everyone, I bequeath them, as well as my mansion, to the Institut de France for the Académie des Beaux-Arts." This was the birth of the museum, created by two generations of art collectors whose temperaments and aims complemented each other. Originally from the Savoy region, the Marmottan family moved to northern France during the reign

Marmottan was an exemplary figure among the bankers of the Industrial Revolution and he was often solicited for advice. He remained mayor of Bruay after 1879, when he was appointed by the government to be chief treasurer and paymaster for the Gironde region. He also worked as an administrator for many companies, including the Lille-Béthune railway line, the coal mines of Ferfay (Pas-de-Calais), the Compagnie immobilière de Paris and the Compagnie générale transatlantique. As his primary concern was to efficiently distribute coal, he actively promoted the Canal du Nord between Lens and Paris.

of Louis XV. The passion for art in this dynasty may have begun with Pierre Marmottan, born in 1780, the son of a pharmacist. An amateur draftsman, Pierre Marmottan twice won awards from the Académie de Valenciennes – in 1799 and again in 1805 – but despite this encouragement, he did not pursue his artistic studies, preferring instead to work in the more sensible field of banking. His son Jules, born in 1829, received a traditional education: after finishing *collège* in Valenciennes, he studied law at the university in Paris and started working with a stockbroker named Mahou. One year later he became a leading partner in Edmond Dollfus' business. The year 1862 was a turning point in his career: he became director of the Bruay coal mining company in the Pas-de-Calais. The situation of the young company at the time was serious: it was heavily in debt and had just lost a costly court case, and only one of the coal pits, the first, was productive. Jules Marmottan courageously devoted all his intelligence and talents to this company. His efforts paid off: within a few years the business expanded and became remarkably successful. The town, which grew from 700 to 6,000 inhabitants in just 20 years, owed a great deal to this benefactor, who also became mayor of Bruay in 1870. Schools, local roads, public baths, relief funds and medical services for workers were created under his leadership. Jules

Left to right:
Tapestry of the
*History of
Saint Susanne*,
(part of a series of
8 tapestries),
French school,
15th century.

School of Lucas
Cranach
(1472-1553),
*Resurrection of
Lazarus*, undated,
oil on wood,
149 x 115 cm.

Hans Muelich
(1515-73), *Descent
From the Cross*,
1536, oil on wood,
150 x 112 cm.

THE MARMOTTAN MANSION

In 1882, one year before he died, Jules Marmottan acquired the mansion facing the Ranelagh gardens. This enclave of greenery was earlier famous for the ball (for which admission was charged) created in 1774 "on the initiative of Lord Ranelagh in London." Even then it was well known as a calm and tranquil park. The mansion was purchased from the heirs of François Kellermann, a maréchal of France who became duc de Valmy in 1808 in recognition of his famous victory. Paul selected a neo-classical design for the office-library, in keeping with his fondness for the Empire style. The sitting rooms and galleries of the future museum perfectly reflect the nineteenth-century spirit; here, like at Chantilly, the furniture, objects and paintings are crowed close together throughout the mansion.

Left to right and
top to bottom:
Paul Marmottan in
his office in 1911.
© Bibliothèque
Marmottan.

Overall view of
the gallery at the
turn of this century.
© Bibliothèque
Marmottan.

The Marmottan
mansion before
the construction of
the side wings.
© Archives
du musée Marmottan.

The Marmottan
Museum today,
viewed
from the garden.

Below: Adrienne-
Marie-Louise
Grandpierre-Deverzy
(active between
1822 and 1855),
*The Studio
of Abel de Pujol*,
1822,
oil on canvas,
96 x 129 cm.

Right, top to bottom:
Etienne Bouhot (1780-
1862), *The Courtyard
of the Institut
de France*, undated,
oil on canvas,
38 x 46 cm.

Louis-Philibert
Debucourt (1755-
1832), *View of
the Arc de Triomphe
and the Grande
Finale of
the Fireworks Display*,
1810, etching
and watercolor,
26 x 37 cm.

On his death in 1883 he left a considerable fortune to his son Paul, as well as a mansion located opposite the Ranelagh gardens he had purchased in 1882 from the Kellermann heirs, and a large collection of artwork. Throughout his entire life, Jules was a well-informed, yet discreet, client of various antique dealers, although he mostly purchased work from Antoine Brasseur, a dealer and art restorer from Lille who worked in Cologne from 1847 to 1887. He accumulated a collection of German, Flemish and Italian primitives. The Haute-Epoque furniture, fifteenth-century wood sculptures and Renaissance tapestries are also in keeping with the austere personality of the collector.

Paul was very different from his father, despite his inherited "passion for order and sense of grandeur." Born in 1856, Paul studied at the Collège de Juilly where he obtained – in reminiscence of his paternal grandfather – the first prize in drawing in 1867. At the age of 18 he decided to travel: he went to Italy

of course, but also to Egypt where he followed in the footsteps of Auguste Mariette, "the eminent antique dealer." By the time he turned 21, he had published his first collection of poems, *Les Primevères*, and was a regular contributor to the *Bulletin administratif, commercial, artistique et littéraire du XVIe arrondissement*, also known as *Paris-Passy*. Nevertheless, under pressure from his father, Paul obtained his law diploma and started working, reluctantly, as an advisor in the prefecture at Evreux in 1882. He admitted that he was "much more interested in the delicate tastes of the artist, the collector and the man of letters than in the troubled areas of politics or the narrow world of the functionary." He did not have to endure this job for long; on the death of his father one year later, he gained his freedom and was able to devote himself fully to his passions: travel and historical and artistic research. He went to Belgium, Holland, the banks of the Rhine, Poland, Spain and Switzerland.

One of the most note-worthy characteristics of Paul Marmottan is that he was interested in the Napoleonic era at a time when others preferred to ignore or even despise it. In his journeys, he was able to accumulate a vast amount of documentation on the subject, works that were added to his considerable library concerning the Empire, including : *le Général Fromentin et l'armée du Nord*, *le Royaume d'Etrurie*, *Bonaparte et la république de Lucques*, *les Troupes de Joseph Napoléon en Espagne*, *Elisa Bonaparte*, *les Arts en Toscane sous Napoléon*, *le Style Empire* and so on. Over the years, he became an expert on art created during the Empire and the Consulate in Paris (and wrote several studies, including *les Statues de Paris* and *le Pont d'Iéna*). This immense library was kept in his home in Boulogne, purchased in 1921; it included thousands of volumes concerning the years from 1799 to 1814. Paul

Above, left to
right, top to bottom:
Empire cups
and saucers,
Woman Giving a
Drink to a Soldier
and *Venus and*
Cupid, undated.

Above: Small round
sitting room
facing the garden;
to the left, the
geographical clock
commissioned
by Napoleon I
Photograph: G. Fessy.

22

Under the influence of Brongniart, appointed to direct the Manufacture de Sèvres in 1800, the production of French porcelain recovered after a period of total decline. Paul Marmottan was particularly fond of Dagoty's designs and purchased a beautiful collection of cups decorated with antique images. The most surprising object, however, is unquestionably the "geographical clock" designed in 1813 in honor of Napoleon I. It was modified during the Restoration and acquired by Louis XVIII, who then gave it to the duchesse de Berry. Napoleon's head was replaced by profiles of Apollo and Diana; and images depicting different time zones decorate the face of the clock, instead of the original design of "twelve subjects in the history of the Emperor."

Top to bottom:
Dagoty, Empire cup and saucer with mythological design, 1804, porcelain, Manufacture de l'Impératrice.

Detail of the face of the geographical clock, 1813-21: twelve painted miniature medallions on porcelain

portray noon in various parts of the world, Manufacture de Sèvres, 2.28 meters high.

Marmottan is an unusual scholar in that it is difficult to separate the historian from the collector. "I arrived at Napoleonic history through art," he said. As opposed to his father, he did not rely on just one dealer, preferring – as he wrote in his book concerning the French school of painting (*l'Ecole française de peinture, 1780-1840*) – to collect his artwork in a more clever way: "When one has acquired an artistic judgment through a combination of personal taste and conscientious study of the old schools, it is not necessary to frequent the large public sales ... It is still possible to find paintings from the French school before 1830 in certain small sales after a death and from certain dealers in curios (who are generally extremely ignorant). In this case, all it takes is a bit of skill to purchase a valuable painting for a low price."

Hector Lefuel, a close friend of Paul Marmottan and first curator of the museum, wrote an introduction to the first catalogue of the collection. In it, he discussed the pride of Paul Marmottan, who "liked to recall the origin of a great number of his works of art made for Napoleon or for the imperial family. Up until the end, he wanted to acquire – to 'save' as he said – the memories of a past for which he felt nostalgia and respect." This passion often meant that he selected the works on the basis of their historical value only, as reflected in the many anonymous views (*A Parisian Street in the Nineteenth Century, The Stables of the Duc d'Angoulême, The Villa de Pline on Lake Como* and so on), or their esthetic interest, such as the surprising eagle clock/vase, which is similar to a piece in the Queen of England's collection. Many well-known artists (Boilly, Kinson, Lefebvre, Bartolini, Prud'hon and Robert) are also included in this unique collection that Paul Marmottan, who died childless in 1932, chose to bequeath to the Institut de France; in this, he may have been inspired by the gesture of Nelly Jacquemart-André 20 years earlier. The Boulogne library and the museum both carry his name, ensuring his posterity; yet he also left a considerable amount of money to Malmaison, the Army Museum, Versailles, Carnavalet, Sèvres, the Costume Museum and the Decorative Arts Museum, as well as to many other museums throughout France. He also left 15 million francs to the Assistance Publique, which added another dimension to this great scholar: that of a true philanthropist. **Laure Murat**

Left to right:
Auguste Renoir
(1841-1919),
*Claude Monet
Reading*, 1872,
oil on canvas,
61 x 50 cm.

Claude Monet
(1840-1926),
*On the Beach
at Trouville*,
1870-71,
oil on canvas,
38 x 46 cm.

The Impressionist Collection

by Sophie Monneret

Donations transformed the Museum – which was originally devoted to Napoleonic history – into a sanctuary of Impressionism. Three bequests to the Académie des Beaux-Arts mark this transformation: one from Victorine Donop de Monchy (Dr. de Bellio's daughter) in 1957; another from Michel Monet (the artist's son) in 1966; and finally, a third from Nelly Sergeant-Duhem (adopted daughter of the painter Duhem) in 1985.

Only part of Dr. de Bellio's collections went to the Marmottan Museum, but the works are superb and include *Impression: Sunrise*, the seminal painting of Impressionism. "Whenever one of us urgently needed money," recalled Renoir, "he ran to the Riche café, where he was sure to find M. Bellio." This Romanian aristocrat came to France during the Second Empire. He practiced medicine only for his friends and collected art with a generous passion. It may have been one of his relatives, Georges Bibesco, for whom Renoir worked in 1869, who kindled Bellio's interest in what was considered to be controversial painting at the time. From Monet in 1874 to Gauguin in 1891, his purchases follow the evolution of Impressionism; the paintings in this collection represent the very essence of the movement. The gift from Michel Monet protrays a discontinuous itinerary through his father's life: portraits (his first wife, his two sons), works by such friends as Jongkind, Renoir and Caillebotte (purchased or gifts) and works from his travels (Riviera, Norway and Holland). The large studies of the Giverny garden complete the excellent collection. They illustrate the creative process in its pure state, at the magical moment when the impression appeared: was it expressionism? or abstraction?

The collection of Duhem and his wife begins with Boudin and continues through the poetic and intimate work of their friend Le Sidaner. Impressionist works, represented in both the virulence of Guillaumin and discretion of Lebourg, hang alongside Symbolist paintings by Carrière. An admirable still-life by Gauguin adds an accent of exoticism to the ensemble.

IMPRESSION: SUNRISE

This immensely famous painting has been mocked, showered with praise and even stolen, but it has always fascinated art lovers. First exhibited during a group show organized in 1874 in Nadar's studio by Monet and his friends, this painting gave its name to the movement that began with this exhibition. Monet, asked to give a title to the work by the editor of the catalogue (Edmond Renoir), suggested "Impression." Renoir added "Sunrise." The satirical newspaper *Charivari* mockingly baptized the style "Impressionism." The canvas (which may have been antedated by Monet), depicts the old harbor of Le Havre seen from the Amirauté Hotel. This painting – a synthesis of watercolors by Turner and Jongkind, as well as the Japanese prints and Chinese ink drawings Money saw in London and Holland – is amazingly modern. First purchased in May of 1874 by Ernest Hoschedé, it was acquired by Dr. de Bellio during a court-ordered sale in 1878.

IN THE COUNTRYSIDE

The fields of flowers
in *Promenade*, filled with
atmospheric notations
and vibrating brushstrokes,
radiate a triumphant
Impressionism. This was
one of Monet's favorite
themes: fourteen
years later, large groups
of wild irises
became pure chromatic
studies. The mauve
and yellow divisionist style
demonstrates that
the painter was concerned
with the neo-Impressionist
style that had
just appeared. And his
anxiety about a
necessary artistic renewal
underlies the moonlit
boat floating
in the current, weighted
down with winding
grasses. Returning to
this project in 1890, Monet
confided in Geffroy
that he was
attempting "impossible
things: water
with grass waving under
the surface. It is
crazy to want to do this."

TRAINS AND STATIONS

Subtle, intangible phenomena such as snow flurries and spiraling curls of smoke always fascinated Monet. *Train in the Snow* depicts the train he took, rain or shine, that ran just a few steps from his second house in Argenteuil. *The Pont de Europe* belonged to the series of Parisian stations, which contained the railway monsters described by Emile Zola. Eight paintings were included in the third Impressionist exhibition; Dr. de Bellio purchased this version. Portraits by Monet are more unusual. He used

Claude Monet,
*Train in the Snow,
The Locomotive,*
1875,
oil on canvas,
59 x 78 cm.

every shade of
blue in the portrait by
François Hippolyte
Guillaume, known as
Poly. Introduced
by Australian painter John
Russell, who lived on
Belle-Isle, this fisherman
from Kervilahouen
showed Monet the
wildest parts
of the coastline in 1886.
Although the artist
exhibited this
superb image several
times, he never sold it.

Top to bottom:
Claude Monet,
Portrait of Poly,
1886,
oil on canvas,
74 x 53 cm.

Claude Monet,
The Pont de l'Europe,
Gare Saint-Lazare,
1877,
oil on canvas,
64 x 81 cm.

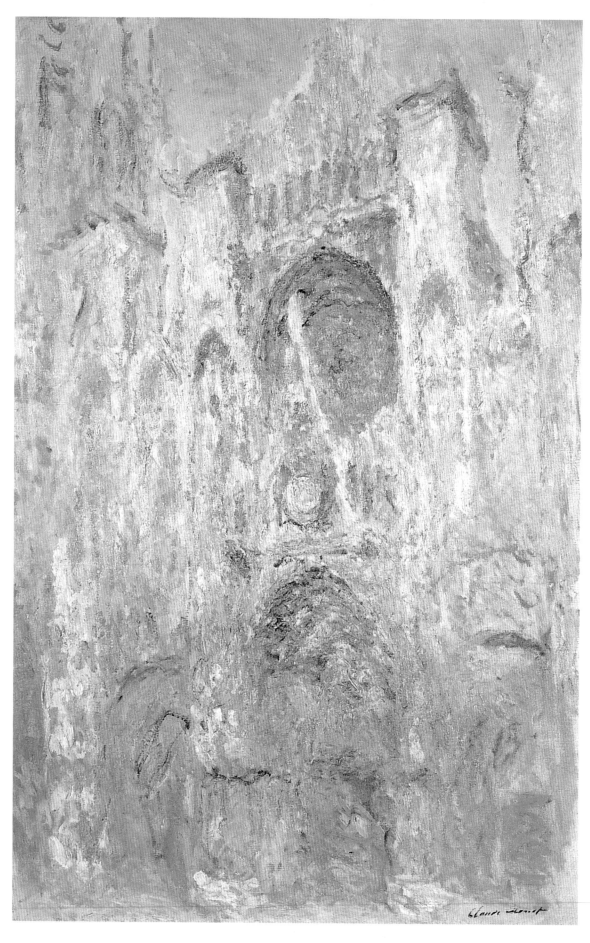

Claude Monet,
*Rouen Cathedral,
Effects of Sunlight,
Sunset*, 1892,
oil on canvas,
100 x 65 cm.

THE ROUEN CATHEDRAL

Top to bottom:
Claude Monet,
*The Seine at
Port-Villez, Evening
Effects*, 1894,
oil on canvas,
52 x 92 cm.

Claude Monet,
*The Seine at
Port-Villez,
Pink Effects*, 1894,
oil on canvas,
52 x 92 cm.

Painted in March and April of 1892 and 1893 in a building located opposite the cathedral, this work was later finished at Giverny. Although dispersed in various collections, the 28 paintings of the *Rouen Cathedral* series represent an entirely novel experiment: the composition is characterized by an abhorrence of empty space and a pictorial material treated as thickly as mortar.

This ambitious project – "colossal work... enormous difficulties" – haunted Monet's dreams. "The cathedral fell on top of me; it seemed to be blue, or pink or yellow." Here the contrast between the shadows and the sunlight on the doors and the Albane tower depict the many effects of dispersed light. Pissarro, Renoir and Cézanne all admired this masterpiece, which was praised by Clémenceau in *The Révolution des cathédrales*. Monet offered an alternative vision to this confrontation with stone in his unfinished views of the Seine at Port-Villez, which appear to be polished mirrors under a gossamer mist.

LONDON FOG

Monet took refuge in London during the war of 1870. There, almost unknown, he painted Westminster Palace, the house of Parliament, from the Victoria Embankment. Thirty years later, rich and famous, he rivaled the work by Turner and Whistler in close to 100 paintings depicting the fog on the Thames. He concentrated on three different themes: *Parliament, Waterloo Bridge* and *Charing Cross Bridge*. Painted from the Saint Thomas Hospital, the parliament has fascinating effects of backlighting. Between the mauve sky and the golden-fringed waves of the river, rises the abstract shape of a ghostly monument with tapered vertical lines, and ultramarine blue striped with emerald green, as modern as any of Rimbaud's cities. *The Waterloo Bridge* was painted from a room in the Savoy Hotel. Some of the pastels reveal the concise design of preparatory sketches in which a few lines suffice to define the arches, the shadows and the swirling water.

Claude Monet,
*London.
The Parliament,
Reflections
on the Thames,*
1899-1901,
oil on canvas,
81 x 92 cm.

WATER LILIES

The *Water Lilies* in the Marmottan collection include several of the numerous variations on this theme painted by Monet in the last third of his life. Annoyed with all the artists who invaded Giverny to paint his favorite landscapes, copying his style, he withdrew to his own plastic universe within an enclosed area. It consisted of two parallel worlds: the flower garden and the water garden. His request to create a pond in the fields of the Epte was sent in 1893 to the *préfet*; in it, he specified that it was to

Claude Monet,
Water Lilies,
1914-17,
oil on canvas,
130 x 150 cm.

be a "pleasure for the eyes," as well as "a decor to be painted." The public discovered Japanese-style gardens during the Universal Exhibitions of 1878 and 1889. The Japanese exhibition organized by Bing in 1886 gave artists the idea of using flowers as a single subject (resulting in Van Gogh's *Sunflowers* and the hydrangea in Montesqieu's poems) and of painting the plant life in ponds. "Can't you go study some aquatic plant?" Pissarro asked his son Georges. The flower chosen by Monet was one of the favorite motifs of

Claude Monet,
Water Lilies, Evening Effects, 1897-98,
oil on canvas,
73 x 100 cm.

the Modern Style.
Nenuphars decorated Gallé
vases, brooches by the
jeweler Vever (a neighbor
of the painter in Vexin),
as well as the candelabras
cast by the Alice Monet's
brothers, the Raingo
family, who created crafted
bronzework. Monet
exhibited the *Water Lilies*
in 1900, but as early
as 1897 he had already
imagined using
the design as a wall decor.
"Juxtaposed, they would
form a room with a
horizon of water." This was
an indirect reply to his
friend Mallarmé, to whom
he was supposed to give
a drawing in 1887 for
La Gloire, in a collection that
also included the *White*

Claude Monet,
Water Lilies, 1903,
oil on canvas
73 x 92 cm.

Nenuphar. "One of those magical closed nenuphars that suddenly enclosed a empty space of intact dreams within its white hollows." The same subject, even closer to the spirit of Mallarmé, reappeared in 1914. Elements and shapes seem to fuse, the grasses spread out like fans and the great snowy cumuli appear to burst from the water while the flowers are created from a cloud. In 1909 Monet exhibited a widely anticipated series called *Water Landscapes*. After diverting the Ru River, an arm of the Epte, the pond was enlarged and many new plants were added. They formed islands that looked like the floral

Left to right:
Claude Monet,
Water Lilies,
1916-19,
oil on canvas,
200 x 180 cm.

Claude Monet,
*Water Lilies
and Agapanthus*,
1914-17,
oil on canvas,
initially
200 x 130 cm,
now 140 x 120 cm.

barges the painter had seen and admired in Holland. The water lilies seem to drift in the shadow of the ash, willows and poplar. "These water landscapes and reflections have become an obsession," confided Monet to Gustave Geffroy in 1908. He was forced to stop painting this theme due to various natural events (a flood in 1910, a cyclone in 1912, which "destroyed the willows I was so proud of") and to bereavement: Alice died in 1911, followed by his son Jean in January of 1914. He was fascinated and consoled by returning to the

Claude Monet,
Water Lilies,
1916-19,
oil on canvas,
150 x 197 cm.

water garden. The plants along the riverbank began to appear in his work, including the cerulean-blue agapanthus. The saturated colors and twisted branches of the willows were inspired from the Ballet Russes. "A restful, energetic whiteness" that appears between the pink and yellow water lilies, framed by the light branches, seems to come straight from *Afternoon of a Faun*. Later, he was hypnotized by the surface of the water itself, and painted circular movements that were in direct contradiction to the work by Cézanne and the Cubists. Monet painted his water lily pond until his death, creating large pieces that, under Clémenceau's influence, entered French museums. Like Chinese poet Tchen Sin Yeou, who wrote *The Garden in a Mustard Seed*, the water lily pond represented the entire universe to Monet.

Claude Monet,
The Water Lily Pond,
1917-19,
oil on canvas,
130 x 120 cm.

Claude Monet,
Water Lilies,
1916-19,
oil on canvas,
130 x 152 cm.

THE JAPANESE BRIDGE

Starting in 1895, Monet began to paint the Japanese footbridge over the pond, a theme he often depicted over the years. The first paintings were very realistic, but in time the bridge became more abstract. The old artist sat to the west of the bridge, facing the wisteria-covered arch, exploring the changes that occurred according to the time of day or the season. He painted this bridge with a stubborn determination that was strengthened by the threat of the cataracts that started to interfere with his vision in 1912. The russet, green and yellow tones in this version (1918) were applied as thickly as on the *Rouen Cathedral* series; it reflects the expressionist style characteristic of the last years of the painter's work. The series devoted to the *Willows* on the northern side of the pond was painted during the war years. In 1917, his friend Mirabeau, a journalist and gardening advisor, died. Debussy, who saw Mélisande's streaming hair in these

trailing branches, died
soon after. These branches
weave a curtain behind
the feminine curve of the
trunk, colored pink
by the light of the rising
sun. When Monet
left the pond, it was to
paint the lime trees
on the northwest side of
the garden. The rose- and
clematis-covered facade
appears beyond the rose
garden. This work was
painted several months
before he underwent an
eye operation; the
exaggerated contrasts, the
furiously entangled
reds and greens, and the
violent color annihilate
the concept of space. In

Claude Monet,
*Japanese Bridge
(The Water Lily Pond)*,
1918-24,
oil on canvas,
89 x 100 cm.

the fiery glow of the
sunset, the Japanese
bridge was reduced to little
more than a rendering
of the two arches,
for the same reasons.
Everything in this
last phase prefigures
the abstract expressionists
who recognized
Monet as their precursor.

Claude Monet,
*The House Viewed
from the Rose
Garden*, 1922-24,
oil on canvas,
81 x 93 cm.

WISTERIA, IRISES AND ROSES

Monet often focused on certain flowers. In his garden, where each and every plant was part of the overall plan. When he was asked to paint the water lily decorations in the Biron *hôtel*, he decided to add a frieze of purple and white wisteria; these were the same flowers that shaded the bridge and festooned the deck. Several years later, after suffering months of color distortions and undergoing three operations on his eye, he regained his sight. He then returned to painting irises, another characteristic flower of the 1900's. He was particularly fond of the Japanese varieties planted around the pond; the tapering leaves and butterfly-like flowers

Right:
Claude Monet,
*Yellow and
Purple Irises*,
1924-25,
oil on canvas,
106 x 155 cm.

Claude Monet,
Wisteria, 1919-20,
oil on canvas,
100 x 300 cm.

blurred the outline of the pond. As for roses, he preferred the simple shapes of the original eglantine, or sweet-briar. This plant had made a spectacular comeback after falling out of fashion for many years. "I spent all summer working with a new feeling of joy," he wrote to the painter Barbier in 1925. This cheerfulness is reflected in the arch of flowers and leaves painted like a cherry branch by Hokusai or an almond tree by Van Gogh. Like Elstir's roses (for which Proust drew his inspiration from Monet), it was "a fair likeness of a portrait of a rose," transposed into this interior garden that contained the art of creation before it appeared on the canvas. From Clémenceau to Paul Valéry and Bérénice, Aragon's heroine, every visitor marveled at the flowerbeds filled with a succession of changing colors "as if the garden was [constantly] repainted."

Claude Monet,
The Roses,
1925-26,
oil on canvas,
130 x 200 cm.

CAILLEBOTTE AND MORISOT

These paintings
by Caillebotte – the most
realistic of the
Impressionists – given to
Monet and kept
in his room until his
death, reflect the
long friendship between
the two artists. *Street
in Paris. Rain,* an extremely
sensitive study for
the painting in the Chicago

museum, represents the
corner of the rue de
Turin and rue de Moscou
near the studio of
their friend Manet.
The Piano Lesson is one of
many paintings
on this theme, depicted in
different styles by
Degas, Manet, Renoir and
Toulouse-Lautrec.
At the Ball, one of Berthe
Morisot's most
classical paintings, was
exhibited at the
second Impressionist
exhibition and
purchased by Dr. de Bellio.
One of the artist's friends,
Puvis de Chavannes,
may have helped
with the sale, as he was
a close friend of
the princess Cantacuzène,
who was related to
the Romanian art collector.

Above:
Berthe Morisot
(1841-95),
At the Ball, 1875,
oil on canvas,
65 x 52 cm.

Center:
Gustave Caillebotte
(1848-94),
*Street in Paris,
Rain,* 1877,
oil on canvas,
54 x 65 cm.

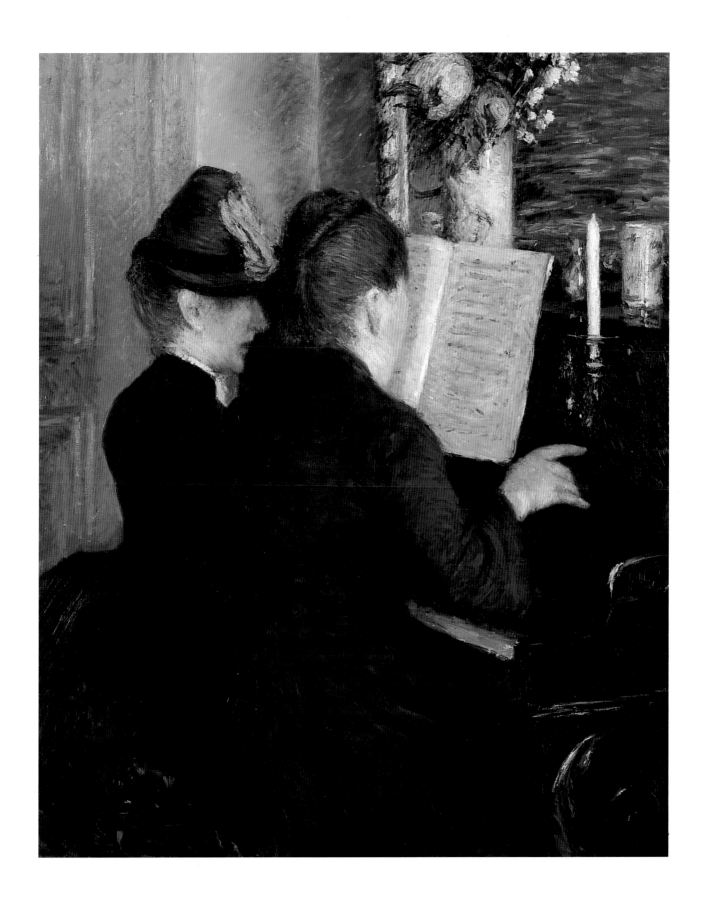

Above: Gustave
Caillebotte,
The Piano Lesson,
1881, oil on canvas,
81 x 65 cm.

Paul Gauguin
(1848-1903),
Bouquet de fleurs,
1897,
huile sur toile,
73 x 93 cm.

GAUGUIN

This masterpiece in the Duhem collection, and one of the rare works by Gauguin from Tahiti in a French museum, illuminates the walls of the Marmottan. It was among the paintings sent in February 1897 to Daniel de Monfreid, a loyal friend who tried to sell the works. *Barbaric Stories*, *Delightful Days* and *The Dream* were also sent with this work, to which Gauguin added a word of advice: to store them "in hope for the day that they decide to pay me properly." The tablecloth and the mangoes reflect Gauguin's interest in Cézanne and the influence of Redon is visible in the transparency to the right. Yet the overall effect of this bowl, sculpted by the artist, reflects his own creative energy. From Tahiti he acquired his "fabulous colors, his sultry, yet filtered and silent ambiance," with which he created these flowers that lie somewhere between reality and imagination.

COROT, SISLEY AND GUILLAUMIN

Above:
Jean-Baptiste-Camille
Corot (1796-1875),
Pond of Ville-d'Avray
Seen Through
the Leaves, 1871,
oil on canvas,
43 x 55 cm.

by Constable in this work, an archetypal Impressionist image: the ephemeral blossoming of the fruit trees under the changing sky of the Ile-de-France. Monet, visiting the poet Maurice Rollinat in 1888, fell in love with the valley of the Creuse. Starting in 1893, Guillaumin came every year. The village of Crozant, the Genetin dam and the gleaming Auvergne autumns all contributed to his development toward expressionism.

Corot prefigured Impressionism, Sisley incarnated the movement and Guillaumin concluded it. Corot, who took refuge in Douai during the Commune, sold this painting to Duhem's uncle. This misty view of the pond close to his country home hangs on the walls of the Marmottan next to works by the Impressionists, who always admired this painter, and near the painting by Berthe Morisot, his student. Sisley, who was extremely sensitive to Corot, was also influenced

Top to bottom:
Alfred Sisley (1839-99), *Spring in the Environs of Paris, Apple Trees in Bloom*, 1879, oil on canvas, 45 x 61 cm.

Armand Guillaumin (1841-1927), *The Creuse at Genetin*, c. 1900, oil on canvas, 65 x 80 cm.

AT THE SEASIDE

The sea and its beaches have been preponderant themes in art since the Second Empire. Boudin, an Impressionist before his time, taught Monet his pictorial techniques. He devoted his life to depicting the visual effects of wind, mist, sails and summer strollers in Sainte-Adresse, Trouville and Honfleur. This is where Baudelaire, in 1859, stood in admiration before several hundred pastel studies "sketched from clouds, the most insubstantial and difficult subject to grasp in terms of form and color." The post-Impressionist generation was also influenced by these works. But the fragmented brushstrokes of Le Sidaner belie the apparent simplicity by creating a underlying mystery, while the linear and modulated definition by Lebasque, a friend of Bonnard and Matisse, reflects a tranquil life of pleasure.

Far left:
Henri Le Sidaner
(1862-1939),
*Clear Morning at
Quimperlé*, undated,
oil on canvas,
73 x 92 cm.

Left: Henri Lebasque
(1865-1937),
*The Pointe
Saint-Gildas*, 1922,
oil on canvas,
65 x 54 cm.

Eugène Boudin
(1824-98),
*Women
and Children on
the Beach*,
undated, pastel,
11 x 28 cm.

RENOIR

Top to bottom:
Edouard Manet
(1832-83),
*Head of a Man
(Claude Monet)*,
1874, India ink
wash, 17 x 14 cm.

Auguste Renoir
(1841-1919),
*Seated Young Girl
With White Hat*,
1884, pastel,
62 x 47 cm.

Above: Auguste
Renoir, *Portrait
of Mademoiselle
Victorine
de Bellio*, 1892,
oil on canvas,
55 x 46 cm.

These three portraits by Renoir all have distinctive characteristics: the somewhat stiff elegance of the future donor, the impertinent boredom of the professional model and the inner tension in the beautiful Camille Monet. In the latest portrait, that of Victorine de Bellio, the artist returned to a more flexible style after a severe Ingres-like period. His skillful use of pastel is clear in this red-haired young girl, an illustration of his favorite theme, adolescence. The portrait of Camille Doncieux, Monet's first wife, was painted during the great period at Argenteuil. It is bathed in the blue shadows that were so highly criticized at the time. The bequest from Michel Monet, born several months before the death of his mother, gives Camille a place of honor among the painters she so often welcomed in her home. Her beauty was enchanting at the time and even today, she still fascinates visitors to the Marmottan Museum.

Above: Auguste Renoir, *Portrait of Madame Claude Monet*, 1872, oil on canvas, 61 x 50 cm.

The Denis and Annie Rouart Foundation

by Marianne Delafond and Caroline Genet-Bondeville

Denis Rouart, grandson of Berthe Morisot, was married to Anne-Marie Conan, to whom the Marmottan Museum owes the honor of this collection of more than 80 works by Berthe Morisot, canvases by Degas, Manet, Monet, Renoir and Rouart, among others. Denis Rouart, curator of the Nancy Museum, lived, like his mother, with the memories of the artist. He and his wife helped to organize exhibitions of Morisot's works, and he wrote several books devoted to her art. Berthe Morisot discovered painting at a very early age. Advised by the best artists, including Camille Corot who taught her about open-air painting, Berthe pursued her passion courageously at a time when the art world was still very much a masculine domain. Wife of Eugène Manet, the painter's brother, she gave birth to her daughter Julie, who became her favorite model. On Manet's request, Renoir made his first portrait of Julie when she was eight years old; she posed with a cat on her lap in the living room of their home. Several years later, he painted the girl again, who, grieving over the death of her father, wore a dress of black velvet. She had many friends in the art world: Puvis de Chavannes, Monet, Renoir and Degas, among others. She maintained a voluminous correspondence with Mallarmé. Most of her close friends were part of the pictorial movement that was created in 1874 during the first Impressionist exhibition. Berthe

Morisot participated in each Impressionist exhibition (except in 1879, after the birth of her daughter) and was considered by her fellow artists to be a "comrade in the struggle." Berthe Morisot's friendship with Auguste Renoir dated to their childhood. Renoir, who participated in the same battle within the Impressionist group, was a loyal companion and a frequent guest at the Thursday evening dinners organized by Berthe Morisot, which included painters, poets and musicians. Berthe Morisot appreciated Renoir's paintings.

In 1886 after visiting his studio, she wrote in a notebook that "in fact, he is a purebred artist, a man of discernment, combined with a fine colorist with the most exquisite sensations. . ." Berthe Morisot died on March 2, 1895. In early 1896, to commemorate her life and work, the "Intransigeants" organized at the Durand-Ruel gallery the most complete exhibition of her art every held. Stéphane Mallarmé wrote the preface to the catalogue, and Degas, Monet and Renoir hung the paintings. The show was a success and was well received by the critics. The journalist Thadée Natanson praised the show in *la Revue blanche*: "Although we have always tried to avoid defining the aspect of a work or some of its qualities with words, for once I have lost this desire. I must abandon the careful stance of describing nothing of the charm and enchantment of it — their bouquets would lost their color and fade."

Berthe Morisot used to go to the Louvre Museum to copy the great masters, and it was there, in 1867, that Fantin-Latour introduced her to the already extremely famous painter Edouard Manet. She greatly admired both his talent and his temperament. As early as 1868, Manet asked her to pose for him. He painted ten intense portraits representing the remarkable beauty of Berthe Morisot. Each one reveals a different facet of the personality of the model — a blend of refinement, violence, melancholy and passion. Manet never painted Berthe Morisot with a brush in her hand, although several years later he gave her the most encouraging possible gift, an easel, as a reflection of the great esteem in which he held her work. They shared a profound friendship, and although Berthe Morisot was not Manet's student, she was certainly influenced by "this bit of new technique," "this new way of painting," which constituted his genius. After the death of Edouard Manet, Berthe Morisot participated actively in the retrospective exhibition held prior to the sale of the master's works, a sale organized by Manet's friend, Théodore Duret, in accordance with the terms of the painter's will.

The year 1874 was a decisive time in the life of Berthe Morisot. She was still greatly distressed by the death of her father at the beginning of the year. She sought refuge in her work, and in the spring decided to abandon the official salons and join the new group of independents artists that had just been created. Invited by Degas, she agreed to hang her work in the large studio of the photographer Nadar, thereby participating in the first exhibition of the Impressionists. On December 22, Berthe married Eugène Manet at the church of Passy, and in 1878 their daughter Julie was born.

Male figures are extremely rare in Berthe Morisot's work, although she did paint her husband several times in the company of their daughter — *Eugène Manet and his Daughter in the Garden of Bougival* is one such work. Julie remained her favorite model, sketched at every age and many times in her notebooks, resting on a sofa inside the house, or perched on a ladder gathering cherries.

Left:
Berthe Morisot,
The Cherry Tree,
1891,
oil on canvas,
154 x 84 cm.

Above:
Berthe Morisot,
*Eugène Manet and
his Daughter in the
Garden of Bougival*,
1881, oil on canvas,
73 x 92 cm.

TRIPS TO NICE

Berthe Morisot loved to travel. She and her husband often escaped Paris in search of new landscapes and new scenes to paint. The afternoon light, the wide open spaces, the lush vegetation, and warm and colorful atmosphere of the south drew the artist to the old city of Nice, which she visited several times. She returned from Nice with several new works, including a few seascapes, such as *The Port of Nice*, painted in 1882 in a confident, almost brutal style. In this unusual composition, the subject is placed at the top of the canvas. Regardless the subject or the material, everything was used for its luminous and emotional qualities. Using pastel and especially watercolor, Berthe Morisot captured ephemeral moments, playing with clarity, colors and the effects of transparencies. Claude Roger-Marx discussed these paintings in an essay: "Nowhere else has Berthe Morisot been so personal, so exquisite, nor has she ever created such a close link between the quality of the instantaneous, quick process and the innate nature of the artist, all totally instinctive."

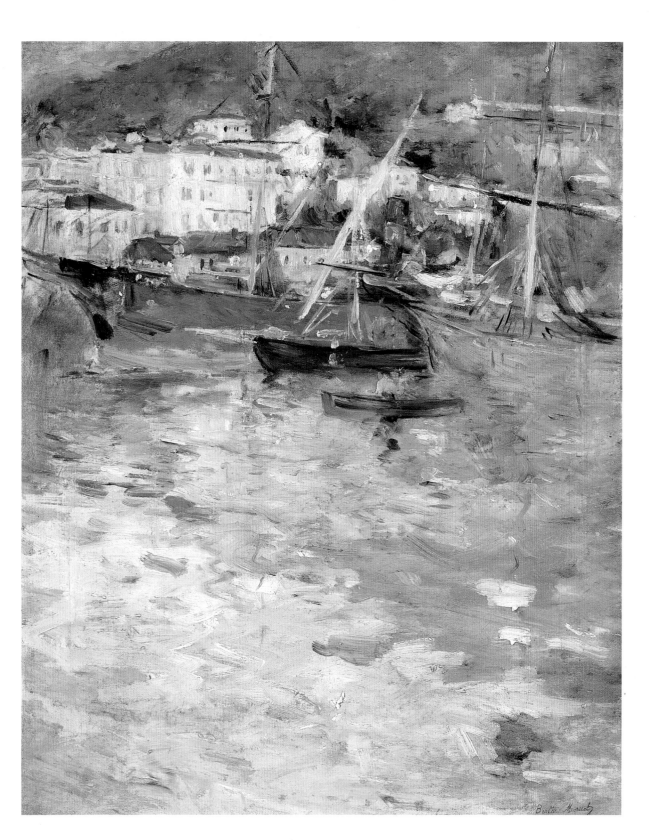

Opposite, top:
Berthe Morisot,
Aloès, villa Ratti,
1889, pastel,
31 x 45 cm.

Opposite, bottom:
Berthe Morisot,
*The Montain
of the Château*,
1888, watercolor,
24 x 31 cm.

Left:
Berthe Morisot,
The Port of Nice,
1882, oil on paper
glued to canvas,
53 x 43 cm.

PRATICAL INFORMATIONS

**Musée Marmottan-Claude Monet
2, rue Louis-Boilly,
75016 Paris.
Tél. 01 44 96 50 33.
Fax 01 40 50 65 84.**

**Open Tuesday to Sunday, 10 am
to 5:30 pm. Guided visits available
by calling 01 44 96 50 33.
Bookstore and museum shop.
Metro: Muette.
Bus: 22, 32, 52, PC.**

BIBLIOGRAPHY

Adler Kathleen and Garb Tamar, *Berthe Morisot*, Oxford, Phaidon, 1987.

Angoulvent Monique, *Berthe Morisot*, Paris, Albert Morancé, 1933.

Bataille Marie-Louise and Wildenstein Georges, *Berthe Morisot*, Catalogue of paintings, pastels and watercolors, Paris, les Beaux-Arts, 1961.

Berhaut Marie, *la Vie et l'œuvre de Gustave Caillebotte*, Paris, Wildenstein, 1951.

Daulte François and Richebé Claude, Catalogue, *Monet et ses amis*, Paris, musée Marmottan, 1977.

Daulte François, *Auguste Renoir, catalogue raisonné de l'œuvre peint, I Figures 1860-1890, II Figures 1891-1905*, Lausanne, Durand-Ruel, 1971-1977.

Delafond Marianne and Genet-Bondeville Caroline, *Berthe Morisot ou l'audace raisonnée*, Denis and Annie Rouart Foundation, Paris, Musée Marmottan, 1997.

Harambourg Lydia, *Dictionnaire des peintres paysagistes français au XIXe siècle*, Neuchâtel, Ides et Calendes, 1985.

Higonnet Anne, *Berthe Morisot, une biographie*, Paris, Adam Biro, 1989.

Huisman Philippe, *Morisot*, Lausanne, Bibliothèque des Arts, Polychrome, 1995.

Lefuel Hector, *Catalogue du musée Marmottan*, Paris, 1934.

Monneret Sophie, *l'Impressionnisme et son époque*, 4 volumes, Paris Denoël, 1978-1981.

Rouart Denis et Rey Jean-Dominique, *Monet, Nymphéas*, Paris, Hazan, 1972.

Rouart Denis and Wildenstein Daniel, *Manet, catalogue raisonné*, 2 volumes, Lausanne et Paris, Bibliothèque des arts, 1975.

Rouart Denis, *Correspondance de Berthe Morisot avec sa famille et ses amis*, Paris, Quatre Chemins, 1950.

Manet Julie, *Journal, 1893-1899*, Paris, Klincksieck, 1979.

Wildenstein Daniel, *Claude Monet*, biography and catalogue raisonné, 5 volumes, Lausanne, Bibliothèque des arts, 1974-1986.

Les Hors Série Beaux Arts magazine sont édités par Beaux Arts SA.

Président-Directeur général :
Charles-Henri Flammarion.
Directeur de la publication :
Jean-Christophe Delpierre.
Rédacteur en chef :
Fabrice Bousteau.
Rédacteurs en chef adjoints :
Caroline Lesage et Stéphane Melchior.
Maquettistes :
Claire Luxey et Fabrice Crélerot.
Iconographe :
Agnès Cuchet.
Secrétaires de rédaction :
Isabelle Arson et Maryse Charlot.
Traduction anglaise :
Lisa Davidson.
Assistante de direction :
Caroline Dubois.

Création et fabrication :
directeur : Alain Alliez,
assisté de Marie-France Wolfsperger.
Marketing :
Isabelle Canals-Noël.
Tél. : 01 56 54 12 35.
Beaux Arts magazine,
33, avenue du Maine,
75755 Paris, cedex 15.
Tél. : 01 56 54 12 34.
Fax : 01 45 38 30 01.
RCS Paris B 404 332 942.
Commission paritaire 65094.
Dépôt légal : juin 1998.
Impression : Berger-Levrault à Toul, France.

Toutes photos : Alban Couturier
sauf mentions contraires.
© Giraudon pour les photos des pages
27, 33, 39, 40-41, 43, 50, 54-55,
56 et de 65 à 73.

Nous remercions pour l'aide qu'ils ont
apportée à la réalisation de cet ouvrage :
Arnaud d'Hauterives, Marianne Delafond,
Caroline Genet-Bondeville et Mauricette
Fallek à la fondation Wildenstein.